birthday Sarah!

What Happens When
Rain
Falls?

What Happens When

Rain Falls?

Daphne Butler

RSVP

RAINTREE
STECK-VAUGHN
PUBLISHERS
The Steck-Vaughn Company

Austin, Texas

Published by Raintree Steck-Vaughn Publishers, an imprint of Steck-Vaughn Company

Library of Congress Cataloging-in-Publication Data

Butler, Daphne, 1945–
    What happens when rain falls? / Daphne Butler.
        p.   cm. — (What happens when—?)
    Includes index.
    ISBN 0-8172-4151-5
    1. Rain and rainfall—Juvenile literature. [1. Rain and rainfall.]   I. Title.   II. Series: Butler, Daphne, 1945–   What happens when—?
    QC924.7.B87   1996
    551.57'7—dc20   95-12061
                                                 CIP
                                                     AC

Printed and bound in Singapore
1 2 3 4 5 6 7 8 9 0 99 98 97 96 95

Contents

It's Raining!   6

Everything Is Wet   8

Down to the Ocean   10

Water in the Wind   12

Rain Clouds   14

Sun and Snow   16

Too Much Rain   18

Too Little Rain   20

Drinking Water   22

Recycling Water   24

Water Power   26

Rain Words   28

Index   30

It's Raining!

Millions of raindrops are beating down onto the ground. They are trickling down window panes and into nooks and crannies.

How does it feel to be out in the rain? What do you wear?

Everything Is Wet

After it rains, roads are full of water. There are puddles, and the grass is covered with water droplets.

What happens to all of this water? Where does it all go?

Down to the Ocean

The rain soaks into the ground.
It gathers into streams. The streams
travel down the hillside. Then they
go into the valleys and all the way
down to the ocean.

The ocean is huge. It covers most
of the Earth.

11

Water in the Wind

Wind that blows over mountains or hills lifts up moisture from the ocean. If the air cools, the moisture turns into clouds.

Not all clouds are the same. Some are thin and float very high in the air. Others are white and fluffy and float much closer to the ground.

Clouds near the ground make up **fog**.

Rain Clouds

Clouds that are dark and flat at the bottom usually make rain. They float high up in the air.

Inside the rain clouds, the wind moves very quickly. It turns the moisture back into droplets of water.

The droplets fall to the ground as rain. Sometimes when it rains, **lightning** flashes.

Sun and Snow

Sometimes, when the sun shines through the rain, you will see a rainbow in the sky.

When it's cold outside, sometimes tiny drops of water will freeze on things during the night. This is called **frost**.

If it is very cold, the rain falls as white, fluffy flakes of snow.

Too Much Rain

When it rains for a long time, rivers may flood. If so, houses and roads may be filled with water.

Very hot countries have a rainy season. During this season, it rains almost every day.

Too Little Rain

When no rain falls, the ground dries out. Cracks appear, and plants die. Their roots can no longer find moisture in the soil.

Some countries are always dry. The land is mostly desert. If plants are to grow at all, they must be watered every day.

The water often comes from wells deep under the ground.

Drinking Water

All living things need water to drink. Without water they will die. People need very clean water. It must be **purified** so that it is free of germs.

Where water is scarce, people save it every way that they can.

In the desert, it is cold at night, and moisture called **dew** forms. It is collected in tall towers.

Recycling Water

Water is too precious to waste. This is true even in countries where there is lots of rainfall.

Extra water is saved in **reservoirs**. It is stored there until it is needed.

Used water is called **sewage**. It is cleaned at sewage farms and then returned to rivers and reservoirs.

Water Power

Water that rushes down a mountain has a lot of energy. People have learned to use this energy.

One way is to build a **dam** across a valley high in the mountains. The water has to run out of the dam through huge tubes.

There are wheels inside the tubes called **turbines**. The water turns the turbines and makes electricity.

Rain Words

dam A huge wall built to hold water back

dew Tiny drops of water that form on things outside during the night

fog Clouds that form close to the ground

frost Frozen dew

lightning Sparks of electricity that flash in the sky during a storm

purify To clean water so that it does not have dirt or germs in it

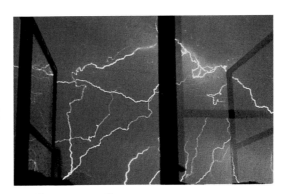

reservoir A place where a large amount of water is stored for future use

sewage Water that contains waste because it has already been used

turbine A kind of engine with a wheel inside it. The wheel is turned by gas, water, or steam.

29

Index

A
air 12, 15, 22
animals 18

C
clouds 12, 15
colors 16

D
dam 27
desert 21, 22
dew 28
dirty water 24
drinking water 22
droplets 9, 15

E
Earth 11, 12

F
flood 18
fog 12
frost 28

G
ground 7, 11, 12, 15,
   21

L
lightning 29

M
moisture 12, 15, 21, 29

O
ocean 10, 11, 12

P
puddles 9
purify 29

R
rainbow 16
raindrops 7, 16
rainy season 18
reservoirs 24

S
sewage 24
snow 16
sun 16

T
turbine 27

W
water 9, 12, 15, 18, 22, 24, 27
wells 21
wind 12, 15

Globe Enterprises © 1993
Published in association with Macdonald Young Books Ltd